BUSINESS BABY

Text by Alex Beckerman and Emily Haynes
with photographs by Ryan Cunningham

Library of Congress Cataloging-in-Publication Data available.
ISBN: 978-1-4521-4259-3

Manufactured in China

MIX
Paper from
responsible sources
FSC
www.fsc.org
FSC® C104723

Designed by Kelly Abeln and Michael Morris
Cover Photograph by Emily Haynes

10 9 8 7 6 5 4 3 2 1

Chronicle Books LLC
680 Second Street
San Francisco, California 94107
www.chroniclebooks.com

BUSINESS BABY

GETTING THINGS DONE, ONE TANTRUM AT A TIME

BY ALEX BECKERMAN

CHRONICLE BOOKS

SAN FRANCISCO

They may not have MBAs or PowerPoint skills, but every parent of a baby knows who's the boss. Someone's in charge, all right, and it's not the person wiping jam off the carpet.

Babies are business wizards. It's only natural: their skill set is perfectly suited for the corporate world. Being unable to do anything for themselves, they're incredibly good at delegating. They're—literally—climbers. And, of course, they give you the business all day long. They're extremely goal-oriented, especially if the goal is to make mommy take a fifteen-minute cry break in the bathroom, just like her real boss used to.

And although their vocabulary is often limited to MINE and NOOOOOO, they're probably just as articulate as many of your previous employers.

Babies think outside the box. Mostly, they think about climbing on the box, or under the box, or how they'd really like you to plop them in the box while towing them around the room shouting HERE COMES THE CHOO CHOO! No, you're definitely not the boss here.

Like any boss, babies are not perfect. They can stick their feet in their mouths (literally). They drop the ball (literally). They poop the bed (literally). In short, they make a mess of things like it's their job. And they're really good at their job.

They're only going to get better, so it's best not to fight it. That kid who's wearing underpants as a hat and trying to eat your car keys is going to run the world someday. So keep your chin up and your head down, and bring the boss his mum-mums before he gets any crankier.

HIGHLIGHT
THIS YEAR'S FINANCIALS?

YOU GOT IT.

SERIOUSLY, A FAX?

THIS WAS OBSOLETE BEFORE MY PARENTS EVEN MET.

COMPANY PICNIC

CRAYON EATING CONTEST!

Games galore:

The Sippy Cup Toss

High Pitch Scream-O-Meter

Tantrum Twister

Food will be provided by:
YOUR MOM
(Seriously, don't forget to bring
her and her cookies)

YEAH, IT'S PRETTY SWEET.

I GOT A RAISE AND, LIKE SIX STICKERS.

OOH, AN INVOICE. BETTER TELL MOM... I MEAN, ACCOUNTING.

JUST LIKE I THOUGHT.

SAYS HERE I'M ALLOWED TO **THROW** MY **SPOON 3X** PER **MEAL.**

SORRY,
CAN'T LOAN
YOU DAVE FOR
THAT PROJECT.

HE'S ON THE
TIME-OUT
CHAIR TODAY.

FILING MY EXPENSES.

WHAT'S THE CODE FOR PLAY-DOH?

BRING ME SAFETY SCISSORS AND SOME GLUE.

I'M GOING TO CUT AND PASTE.

BEST OFFICE TOYS

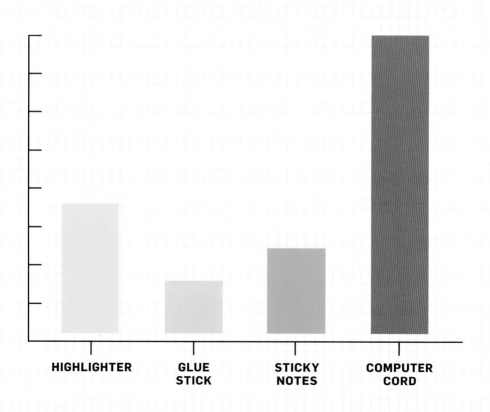

HIGHLIGHTER   GLUE STICK   STICKY NOTES   COMPUTER CORD

TOO MUCH ON MY PLATE, AND I DON'T KNOW HOW TO USE A FORK.

JUST SAW A **BABY DANCING** LIKE **BEYONCÉ.**

THAT'S ENOUGH **INTERNET** FOR TODAY.

I HATE MY COMPUTER. IT KEEPS PLAYING OLD McDONALD.

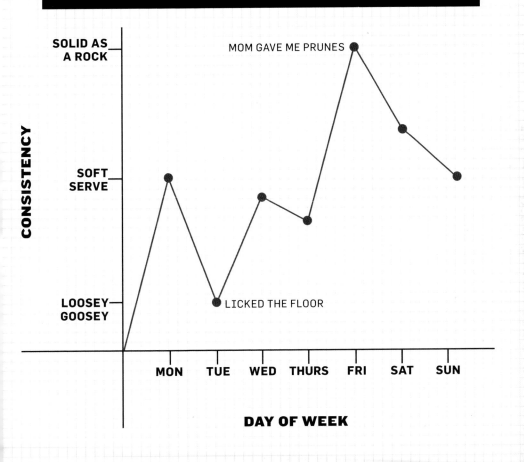

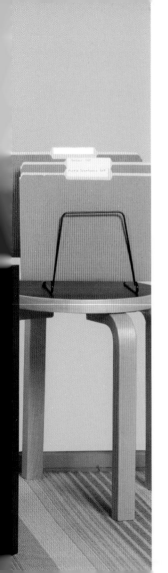

PULL IT *TOGETHER,* JOSEPH. SOMEONE WILL FIND YOUR BINKY.

FEBRUARY INVENTORY

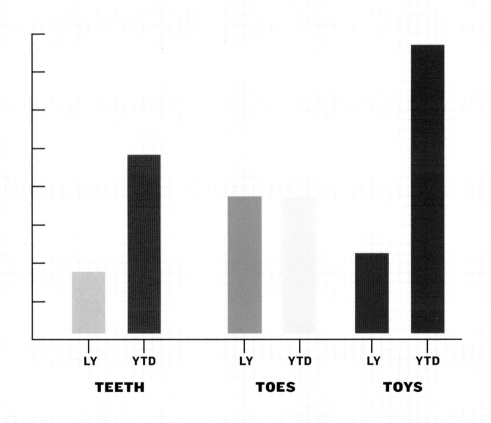

	LY	YTD		LY	YTD		LY	YTD
TEETH			**TOES**			**TOYS**		

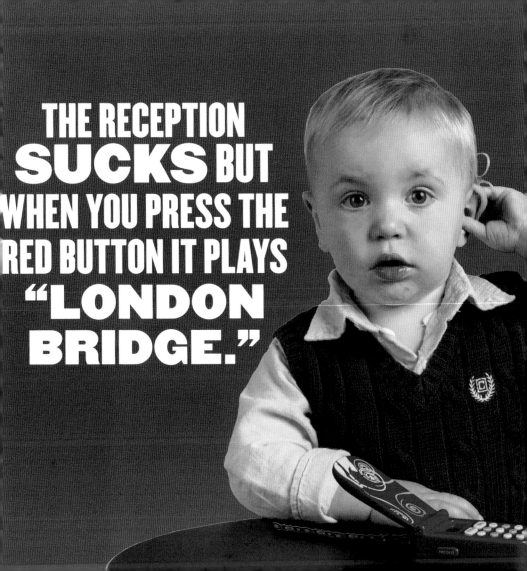

IF WE **WEREN'T SUPPOSED TO**

PLAY **BUMPER CARS,** THEY WOULDN'T HAVE **WHEELS.**

CHECK THE
BREAK ROOM SINK,
STAT.

THE ITSY-BITSY
SPIDER'S BACK!

YOU DIDN'T GET THE *JOB.* **APPLY AGAIN WHEN YOU'RE** *THIS MANY.*

I DON'T KNOW WHAT EXCEL IS,

BUT I ALREADY HATE IT.

IF I'M NOT SUPPOSED TO STICK IT IN MY NOSE, WHY IS IT SHAPED LIKE A FINGER?

CLARIFY WHAT?

THIS IS CLEARLY A PIE CHART.

IT'S FIVE O'CLOCK SOMEWHERE.

TIME TO BREAK OUT THE SIPPY CUPS.

EFFECTIVENESS OF A TANTRUM

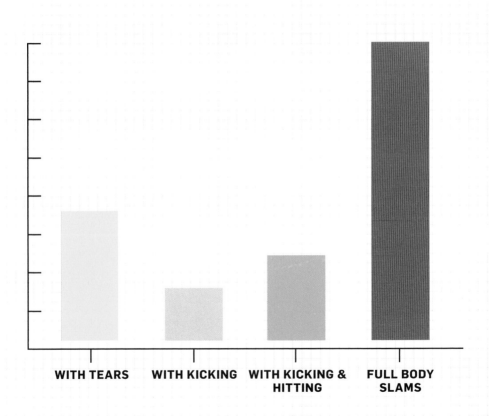

WITH TEARS   WITH KICKING   WITH KICKING & HITTING   FULL BODY SLAMS

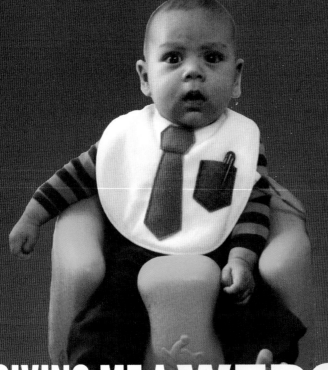

KITCHEN PSA

YOUR MOM *DOES* WORK HERE SO MAKE A MESS!

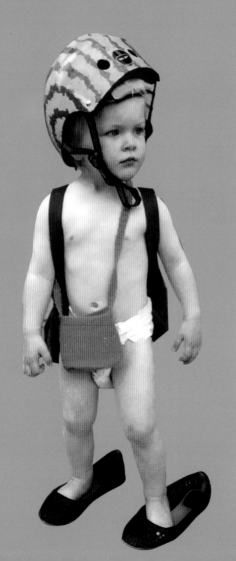

DON'T JUDGE ME.

IT'S BIKE TO WORK DAY.

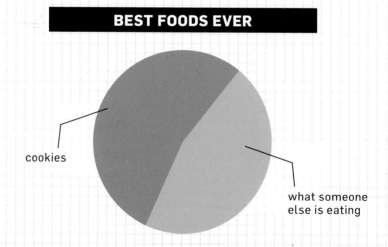

KEEP
CALM
AND
TAKE
A NAP

The More
You Share,

the Less
You Have

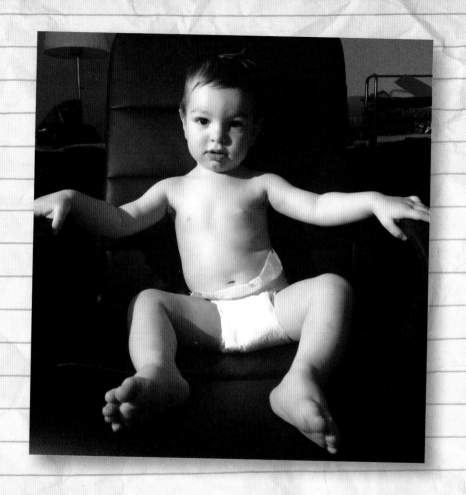

I WEAR THE **PANTS** IN THIS OFFICE.

NO,
I DON'T KNOW WHO PUT A **HALF-EATEN** GRAHAM CRACKER IN THE **COPIER.**

BUT IF YOU FIND IT I WANT **IT BACK.**

PRODUCTIVITY WOULD PROBABLY INCREASE IF WE

GOT RID OF THE CEILING FAN.

CAN YOU **BELIEVE** *HE* GOT PROMOTED?

HE DOESN'T EVEN KNOW HOW TO **WAVE BYE-BYE.**

IT'S COOKIE MONSTER.

HE'LL BE NEGOTIATING MY LUNCH MENU.

COMPANY SANDBOX RULES:

THE COMPANY SANDBOX IS OPEN FROM **3 P.M.–5 P.M.**

NO OFFICE SUPPLIES

NO POOPING

NO CATS

NO THROWING SAND

I'LL **CONSIDER** YOUR PROPOSAL,

ONCE YOU'VE **BROUGHT ME**
MR. BUNNY

HE MIGHT HAVE MISUNDERSTOOD WHAT **I MEANT** BY BOTTOM LINE.

I CAME HERE TO DO TWO THINGS: **WATCH CARTOONS, AND FIRE PEOPLE. LOOKS LIKE I'M JUST ABOUT *OUT OF CARTOONS.***

IF I HEAR THE WORDS "GROSS MARGIN" ONE MORE TIME I'LL STICK THIS PHONE CORD UP MY NOSE

IT'S **HANDS-FREE** IF

I **PUSH** THE **BUTTONS** WITH MY **TOES**.

HOW TO WHINE

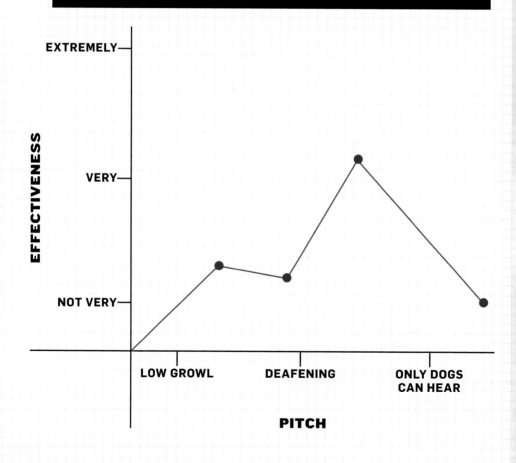

WHO IS THIS
NIGERIAN PRINCE

AND WHY CAN'T HE SPELL?

OH,
YOU ACTUALLY
THOUGHT
I CARE
ABOUT YOUR
CARPAL
TUNNEL
SYNDROME?

NOT WHAT YOU MEANT BY "KEEP ME IN THE LOOP"?

EMPLOYEE HANDBOOK
TABLE OF CONTENTS

I HAVE NO IDEA **WHAT KEY**

MAKES THE **WAFFLE** COME BACK OUT.

SHARING PSA

Number	Author	Title	Publisher	Date	Source	Co
01						
02						
03						
04						
05						
06						
07						
08						
09						
10						
11						
12						

If you chew on a pen, it's yours.

If you stick it up your nose, it's yours.

If you stick it in your diaper, it's DEFINITELY yours.

Otherwise, please share.

YEAH, IT'S KIND OF **BIG** FOR A CELLPHONE.

BUT THE '80s ARE BACK.

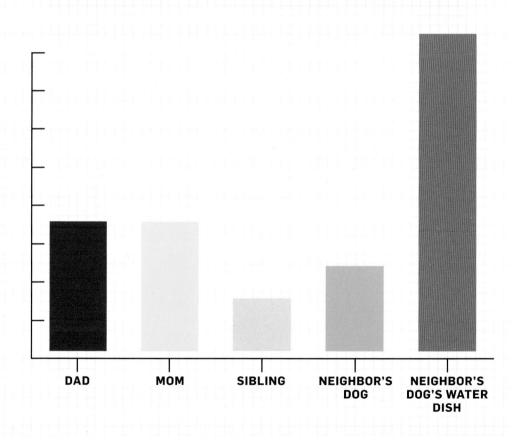

BETTER CALL MAINTENANCE.

I MADE BOOM-BOOM.

CASUAL FRIDAY IS FOR

LOSERS.